Women Empowering Women

Break the Mold and Make a Difference

Dr. Deidre Anderson

Trindalin Browning

Sandra German

Tracie Randolph

Melissa Simmons

Candi Stewart

Shema Stroud

Women Empowering Women
Break the Mold and Make a Difference

©2017 by Dr. Deidre Anderson, Trindalin Browning, Sandra German, Tracie Randolph, Melissa Simmons, Candi Stewart, Shema Stroud

ISBN: 978-0-9894364-4-1

Library of Congress Control Number: 2017954062

Printed in USA by Dr. Deidre Anderson

Published by Business Authority Press

The authors and publisher have strived to be as accurate and complete as possible in the creation of this book. In practical advice books, as in anything else in life, there are no guarantees of results. Readers are cautioned to rely on their own judgment about their individual circumstances and to act accordingly.

The advice and strategies found within may not be suitable for every situation. This work is sold with the understanding that neither the authors nor the publisher are held responsible for the results accrued from the advice in this book.

While all attempts have been made to verify information provided for this publication, the publisher assumes no responsibility for errors, omissions, or contrary interpretation of the subject matter herein. Any perceived slights of specific persons, peoples, or organizations are unintended.

Dedication

This book is dedicated to all the courageous women ready to step out, break the mold, and make a difference in the world by helping each other.

This book is for all the women looking for inspiration to keep going when the days are dark. When we are faced with obstacles and situations that challenge both our spirits and hearts, we all need practical guidance to help us navigate our way forward, knowing that the transformation gained enables us to help others going through similar situations.

May you find in these pages encouragement, hope, and new insights to help you move forward, regardless of what is happening in your life right now, with a renewed commitment to continue learning, growing, and making our world a better place.

Acknowledgements

The creation of this book has been a labor of love with many contributors to "birth" it from idea to reality.

First, we want to thank our amazing clients who have validated (via the results in their own lives) that the concepts, ideas, and advice inside this book are life-changing. Without them, this book would never have been written.

Thanks to all our mentors, teachers, and colleagues who lead and taught us by not only their words but by their example of what is possible.

We are grateful for all the hands and hearts who touched this book by way of polishing the content, creating the cover, laying out the design, and guiding us to the finish line.

Contents

Introduction
Dr. Deidre Anderson

I turn my head to peer out of the window as our pilot announces our descent into Cancun. Staring into the shimmering blue-green waters, I feel my heart race with anticipation. This is not my first time visiting the white sand beaches of this tropical paradise, yet here I sit, perched on the edge of my seat with wide eyes and a girlish grin that remind me of a five-year-old on Christmas morning.

"We'll never be the same," I predict, as the plane touches down and the passengers offer the pilot a round of applause.

There is nothing extraordinary about the landing, but there is something life-changing happening for the 27 women who have traveled to this sun-drenched utopia along the Yucatan Peninsula, literally holding their lives in their hands. We are all here to participate in Women Empowered's first destination retreat – and every woman has in her possession a personalized Launching ME Life Plan, created after six months of painstaking effort.

This one-of-a-kind tribe is far from being a group of casual vacationers. When we step off of the plane, we bring with us a shared history and a special mission that connects us through an inextricable bond. For half a year, we have laughed together, cried together, and encouraged one another along the journey, as each of us designed a customized roadmap to guide our steps towards intentional living. Our arrival in Cancun not only represents a chance to celebrate a remarkable achievement, it also marks a rare opportunity to witness and affirm the declaration of one another's life goals against the awe-inspiring backdrop of the Caribbean Sea.

These ladies – just over two dozen in number but far more powerful in strength – are the courageous trailblazers who birthed a movement charged with daring women to break the mold and make one another better. Each of them has made significant contributions to this world, including the six women who wrote this book.

As the executive director of Women Empowered (W.E.), I am honored that the authors invited me to write an introduction for this wonderful publication. I could not be more proud of each of them and the transformation that has taken place in their hearts and minds over the past few years.

This book provides a rare glimpse into the lives and philosophies of six extraordinary women who refused to shrink back and give up despite the tremendous challenges that they have endured. For some, it is the first time that they have shared their stories publicly. Yet, inspired by W.E.'s vision of a world in which women make one another better, they have mustered the courage to transform their pain into a platform that offers help and healing to others going through similar situations.

In each of the book's chapters, you will hear the story of the author told in her own unique voice. You will gain insight into topics such as dealing with a life-threatening illness, reclaiming your career, and redefining what it means to be beautiful. Every section of the book will leave you feeling inspired and ready to take action. Not only that, this book also invites you to join the Women Empowered movement and link arms with us. Each of the authors in this book is a certified Launching ME Life Plan mentor who can help you walk through completing and implementing your life plan and overcome the obstacles that you will face in trying to do so.

I trust that you will enjoy learning about the fascinating life experiences of these exceptional women. These authors have not only shared openly about their struggles, but, in the spirit of true pioneers, they have offered practical guidance to help you navigate through similar terrain. It is my hope that what you read will not only inspire you, but compel you to also take action.

Is it time to link arms with a down-to-earth tribe of women that you know will support and encourage you in your efforts? Are you ready to step out, be bold, and take action in order to fulfill your dreams? Do you want to finish what you have started and begin living your life more intentionally? Have you been searching for someone who can identify with the unique challenges you are facing and help you over life's hurdles? Then, you have picked up the right book.

About Dr. Deidre Anderson (Dr. D) & Women Empowered

Dr. Deidre Anderson is the founder of Women Empowered (W.E.), a non-profit organization designed to help women become the best leaders they can be. The mission of W.E is to create a movement that dares women to break the mold and its vision is a world in which women make one another better.

This community of lifelong learners promotes healing and wholeness by encouraging women to grow in their leadership, affirm one another's gifts, and support one another in their journey. The organization strives to encourage women to step out, be courageous, and take action in order to fulfill their dreams. W.E. also encourages women to share what they learn to help others advance and to give back to the local and worldwide community.

Fueled by a passion to help women be the best leaders they can be, Dr. D combined her extensive training and coaching background with her doctoral research in the field of strategic leadership and change management to create a stellar program just for them. She teaches three tenets of leadership, the ABCs – Authenticity, Boldness and Change – through her TransformHer Women's Leadership Program.

Dr. D's belief is that when women lead authentically and boldly, everything in and around them changes; they transform their families, communities, workplaces and the world – from the inside out. She encourages women to join this powerful sisterhood of women who inspire, support and empower one another to dream big, reach high, and become the change this world needs.

Each year, Dr. D leads women on a journey of transformation that includes six months of small group coaching. The program culminates with a destination retreat and Women's Conference. W.E has established an international presence, traveling to worldwide destinations including Paris, Punta Cana, Italy, Greece, and Cancun.

Go to WomenEmpoweredInternational.com to learn more. To receive W.E.'s latest updates and words of inspiration, visit Women Empowered International on Facebook (https://www.facebook.com/Women. Empowered.International/). Email us at info@women-empoweredinternational.com.

Chapter 1

Discover Your True Beauty and Passion from the Inside

Sandra German

"Mom, oh my god, your room is on fire!" my son shouts. I think he's joking, because he is a jokester. "Jules, stop telling stories," I reply calmly. My son continues to insist that, even though he's been downstairs doing his homework while I ran out to the cleaners around the corner, he hears crackling coming from upstairs.

I walk upstairs and find my room is engulfed in flames. "Get the dog!" I call to my son and grab my purse and car keys. Once assured they are safe, I scramble to save the only other thing I can. I pull my car out of the drive-way. From across the street, I see the windows in my house start to pop out. The fire department arrives and so does my estranged husband, from whom I had managed to finally separate after years of infidelity.

I have learned that disaster doesn't always strike suddenly; sometimes it eats away at you for years before you even notice it. My ex-husband sweeping back into my life in the aftermath of the fire was just as devastating as the blaze that ravaged the home we once shared.

When we married, I was twenty three and, like many women, I thought I had found my Prince Charming. Imagining our future together, I dreamed of a life filled with exciting new possibilities. I was in my last year of college, scheduled to graduate in May, newly married and excited to find myself pregnant, expecting our first child. Reality crashed in when I had a miscarriage at 5 months, just 2 months before I was due to graduate. I was devastated by the loss of my pregnancy and disappointed to have to push back my graduation date until August, but grateful to have that accomplishment completed.

A year later, I became pregnant again. The second pregnancy was very difficult. At two months, I went to the doctor for what I thought was a routine checkup. While I knew something wasn't quite right, I was dumbfounded to discover I was losing the baby; the same complication that happened with my first pregnancy was happening again. After having an emergency procedure, I was able to carry the baby full term on strict bed rest the entire time. I gave birth to a healthy baby boy, my son Jules.

I had moved directly from my parents' home into a home with my husband. I never lived on my own and learned how to take care of myself in the world. Even though I worked outside the home sporadically, I was very dependent on my husband. Despite this dependence, I felt my life was complete. I had married a young man who had a very promising career ahead of him. I had a beautiful baby boy, and the luxury to stay at home to care for him.

The trouble with my marriage materialized suddenly. I received a phone call from a young lady who claimed that she was my husband's girlfriend. When I approached him about this, I got the classic responses: "I don't know what you're talking about." "I can't imagine who would do something like this." "Just ignore it." With his career, he was frequently away from home. Over the next several months, the young lady continued to call and tell me stories about places they had been and things about him that I knew were true.

I began looking for a job, with the intention of leaving him. My son was only a year old and I was scared of what might lie ahead for both of us. I set aside my plans after my husband convinced me that he wanted our family to stay together and that he loved me. He proposed a move from Philadelphia to New Jersey to "get away from all of this" and begin again. I was young and naïve, so I agreed. I believed I still loved him and allowed myself to be convinced of his love for me. And truthfully, I did not know how I could take care of myself and our son.

For several years, life seemed to be good. My husband was successful and together we built a lifestyle that was comfortable; however, the same familiar, disruptive behavior began to gradually emerge again. My husband was away from home constantly, either entertaining clients or traveling for his job. I began finding receipts from hotels. Several friends approached me about seeing him out with other women. The accusations and recriminations were debilitating; my sense of self-worth plummeted. My husband's accusation that I would never be able to make it on my own mirrored my own fears. I was so lost, not knowing who I really was after all these years of turmoil, pain, and dependency.

One Friday the weight of all this finally hit me. Although I had no idea how I was going to financially afford to be out on my own, I knew I had to get out of this toxic relationship. I was working at the time. My son was in elementary school. The time was right. I reached out to a friend who offered us a place to stay. Over the weekend, I packed up our belongings. I contacted a moving company to arrive after my husband left for work and my son left for school.

My son and I were finally away from the constant turmoil. I only shared that "Your father and I are not really seeing eye-to-eye. Sometimes, that's what happens." We stayed with my friend for about 6 months until, slowly, I was able to build a life for my son and myself.

We were separated for close to three years. Although we hadn't divorced, we were living separate lives. It was the chaos and trauma of the house fire that brought us back together again. The fire was caused by an electrical fault that had smoldered in the walls right behind where

I laid my head at night. We all sat there for hours as we watched the house burn down to the ground.

Losing the pictures of my son, his toys and the gifts he had made for me was heartbreaking. The loss of the evidence of the life I had built for my son and myself left me bewildered, as frightened and unsure as I had been when I left my husband three years before. My ex-husband offered us a place to stay while the house was rebuilt. I agreed. My family was far away, and his offer would allow me to keep my son in the same school.

The house took about a year to rebuild. During that time, we attempted to rebuild our relationship. I was working from home one day and realized my husband had accessed his email but had not logged out. Something told me to look through the emails. I discovered that he had an 8-month-old son that he never told me about. There were emails from several women — and one of them was a woman he had had an affair with for over 10 years. The final straw came when 2 airline tickets arrived in the mail for him and his mistress. Two weeks later, I filed for divorce and I never looked back.

For so many years, I had struggled to believe the fantasy of a perfect marriage and family. All the while, my husband's words and actions made me feel like I was a lesser person and that I needed him to survive. I was convinced that I would never amount to anything unless I stayed with him. This is what kept me in the situation for so long, and prompted me to return to him repeatedly as I just existed with no real purpose or joy in my life.

It wasn't until that last breakup, when I filed for divorce, that I finally took stock of my life. The healing process required a lot of soul searching and doing my own personal development work. I realized that each separation made me stronger and fostered my sense of independence. These experiences really helped me discover who I am as a person and made me realize that I didn't need anyone to define who I am as a woman.

True Beauty Comes from Within

True beauty is not what others see on the outside; it is that passion and burning desire that we have from within. One of the greatest gifts that we can give ourselves is to really love ourselves and nurture those gifts that we've been given. Only then can we freely give these gifts away so that we can make an impact. When we lock into our gifts, a whole new world opens up. We know we are operating from our divine purpose and it radiates on the outside. Only after I was able to really see and own that my purpose is to help others did I find my own true inner beauty.

Throughout all the turmoil of my marriage, I maintained a facade. It's one thing to look the part on the outside. It's a whole different ballgame when we are able to really live out the purpose and mission that we know in our heart of hearts we are destined to do. It was only after I discovered my true purpose, healed from the emotional scars, and stepped into my calling that I became whole and free. I was finally able to understand my role and the significance that I had in this world. I have found that life's trials and tribulations are often blessings in disguise.

I am now using my gifts to help women discover their true worth and value. It may be something that circumstances or situations in the past have stolen from them as they did me. When we are sure of who we are and can truly love ourselves, we realize there's no limit to what we can accomplish. "Owning your own story and loving ourselves through the process is the bravest thing we can do." – Brene Brown

I was in my 40s when I finally discovered the path to claim my true beauty, on the inside and the outside. I began living my purpose - free of emotional turmoil - and finding real joy in my life. I learned to love myself and take the needed steps to move on and create the life I am here to live and to help those I am called to help.

Beauty isn't a look, it's a feeling. I love this quote from Ellen DeGeneres, "True beauty is not related to what color your hair is or what color your eyes are. True beauty is about who you are as a human being, your principles, your moral compass." It's about knowing and accepting who you are and can only be revealed from that light shining from within. That light comes from knowing what your purpose is in life and having a desire to fulfill that purpose. How many of us stop to consider that our outer layer is merely a reflection of inner processes? Beauty is being the best possible person - on the inside and out.

Here are the five steps any woman can follow to find her true inner beauty and change her life.

Five Steps for Discovering Your True Beauty

1. Discover who you are and love yourself first.

Regardless of whether we are young or old, the first step is to discover who you truly are as a woman and to first love yourself. That is the only way we can truly love and serve our families, our communities, and those we are here to help. It starts by allowing yourself to have some quiet time to reflect on your life. Every experience, good and bad, has shaped you into being the person that you are today. Were you able to endure the storm? Then you have strength. Did you give up? If not, you know how to persevere. What do you desire and what mark do you want to leave on the world? If you left this world today, what would people say about you? These are the questions that help us find our purpose and claim our strength. This is a process.

Your process may be different from someone else's, but trust the process and know that it will eventually take you where you need to be. It's through exploration that you find that which makes your heart beat and brings out that fire that burns within. When you allow this to happen, you become more in tune with yourself and what it is you are passionate about. Don't be afraid to tell your story and to become transparent.

Being transparent will allow you to grow, push beyond your now, and shift to your next. People are more receptive to those who are able to share their experiences; it makes them seem more human. It will allow others to feel free to open up to expose those things that might be holding them back from discovering who they truly are.

2. Seek your true purpose.

Many times, we stray from our path when life's challenges and day-to-day tasks demand our attention. It may be hard to view the adversity that arises as a true gift that will teach us valuable lessons. All the years of turmoil with my marriage certainly taught me many lessons that I now look back on as gifts and stepping stones for discovering what I am here to do, my real purpose. It all starts with a decision that we not only want but are willing to pursue our calling, even if it means going after something different.

In order for any of us to move forward, we must create a clear picture or vision of what we truly want. When we imagine what we want our life to be like a year, 5 years or even 10 years from today, we get excited and motivated. The desire for what you want your life to be will propel you to live out your dream and fulfill your purpose.

3. Develop your plan for moving forward.

Create short-term goals that are attainable and build toward your ultimate goal. Your plan will then contain the steps necessary to achieve your goals. The steps must be broken down into manageable pieces so we actually see our progress as we accomplish the first steps. Our confidence grows as we continue to take action and see results, no matter how small or large they may be.

4. Create a tracking and monitoring process.

As we begin to take action toward what we truly want, challenges will arise and setbacks may happen. Remember that obstacles are not a reason to give up and stop. They are sometimes put there because there is something we need to revisit, learn, or tweak in our plan. We can learn to take those bumps in the road in stride and keep pushing forward.

If something comes up that prevents us from sticking to the plan, we can take a closer look and assess why and make adjustments so we can keep moving. If we find ourselves stuck and unable to take any action, reminding ourselves of that big vision and goal can help us get back in the game and keep moving.

Sometimes what we initially set out to do doesn't work. There is always another way. Even if plan A didn't work, we can define our plan B.

5. Seek help to make your vision a reality.

Most of us need help as we begin to move forward. We need an objective perspective to brainstorm ideas and help us define the most important first steps. Trying to find answers without any advice or guidance will likely lead to frustration and a lack of progress.

Next Success Steps

Making a decision to create the life, career, relationships, or business we truly want is the first step. When we start by learning to love ourselves and knowing that anything we want to do or create is possible, our lives change as our inward beauty shines outward.

We may find ourselves in challenging circumstances (as I did with my marriage) and feel lost and adrift in the sea of obstacles that are thrown our way. Understanding who we truly are and discovering our purpose, and knowing we have the freedom to make choices and to create what we truly want in life is critical to our success. "Success is knowing your purpose in life, growing to reach your maximum potential and sowing seeds that benefit others." -John C. Maxwell

If you are a woman searching to clarify your purpose and to identify a path to move forward, please email me at sandy@womenempoweredinternational.com to get more information and set up your complimentary 30-minute Inner Beauty breakthrough call.

About the Author

Sandra German earned her Bachelor's Degree in Social Work from Temple University and has worked in the field of Social Work for over 25 years. Through her professional experience, Sandra developed a love for helping people and making them feel good. She has assisted countless individuals in overcoming barriers in their personal and professional lives. Helping people was the driving force behind Sandra's inspiration to become a life coach.

A certified Life Coach and Image Consultant, Sandra is on a mission to help women discover their passion and true beauty from the inside out. She is the founder and creator of Skin Deep Life Coaching and Image Consulting and Iamskindeep, a program that promotes self care as a tool for equipping women to define their true purpose in life. In addition, Sandra offers individual and group coaching sessions as well as workshops to inspire women to pursue their passion and climb to greater levels of success. She truly believes that the greater in you ignites when you discover what sets your soul on fire!

Sandra is the mother of a 23-year-old son, Jules German. She enjoys life to the fullest, and her love for music takes her to a happy place. A resident of Cherry Hill, NJ, Sandra values quality time spent with family and friends.

Chapter 2

Overcoming Adversity: 8 Steps for Turning Challenges into Lessons that Can Change Your Life

Candi Stewart

Stepping alone off the huge airplane, I am excited to be in America. My nine-year old eyes can hardly take in the size of the plane and the vastness of the Boston Logan Airport.

I am following my grandmother to the United States to be reunited with my mother, whom I haven't seen in six years. I was raised by my grandmother, and we have traveled together to Lisbon from Cape Verde Island, a former colony of Portugal off the coast of Africa. My grandmother came ahead, and I was left in Portugal to wait for my visa. So, now I am traveling alone. I am coming to a whole new world called America. I am also coming to a family that I really don't know well. Will I even recognize my mother when I finally see her? I don't know the man she has married, who is now to be my stepfather. My aunt left the island when I was very young, as well. Will she know who I am when we meet? I am filled with fear.

I look around the airport and see no familiar faces. Every other person is greeted by someone. Since I speak only Cape Verdean and Portuguese, I do not understand what anyone is saying. I am adrift in a completely new environment, one I had never seen or experienced before. As the crowd diminishes, my anxiety grows more intense and I realize I am all alone in this very strange new place. My eyes well up with tears. I can hardly breathe.

Finally, when no one else is left in that section of the airport, I try to relay my distress to a female employee. Since I cannot speak English, after a few attempts to understand who I am and why I am here alone in the airport, she finds a man who speaks Cape Verdean. I give him my name and he asks for the names of people in my family. He doesn't seem to know my family, but, as I give him different names, he finally recognizes one.

The man gets someone on the phone who knows my family and instructs me to come with him and his wife. Here I am, a very fearful nine-year-old girl, getting in a car with people I don't know. Yet they speak my language and, with no other options, I agree, not knowing where I'm going.

Let me offer a note of explanation. This was March, 1975, when the main communication method was telephone or telegram. There were no cell phones or tablets with easy access to anything we need to know. I later learned that the telegram providing all the details of my trip was never received by my family; however, none of this was clear to me at the time.

In due course, the car arrives in East Boston. I finally meet my mother and my stepfather. Although they are happy to see me, and I am relieved to get to my destination, all I can think is "Oh, my God. I want to be with my grandmother back in Cape Verde. I'm never going to be able to adjust and fit in. I'm not going to learn the language. How will I survive this?" The dream of America being a wonderful, great place to live is totally shattered and all I feel is fear.

From this jarring, disturbing start in America, my journey of learning how to overcome adversity began. Here are the eight key steps I discovered for turning a challenging life situation or adversity into lessons that can change your life.

Eight Steps to Overcoming Adversity

1. Watch your self-talk and reframe the negatives.

What we focus on is what we empower. Our own voice is the loudest voice, the most powerful voice. So watch what you tell yourself. For many years, I told myself I can't do it. I'm not good enough. I am a mistake that my mother regrets. But there was something in me that wanted to believe differently. It wasn't until I was in graduate school years later that I recognized how much power my words had. With help from pastors, teachers and counselors, I started to take baby steps towards thinking more positively. It's still a struggle today at times, but I am so much further than I would have been had I not embraced the truth that my self-talk is significant to my success. The Bible says, "As a man thinks so is he." (Proverbs 23:7)

This concept was introduced to me when I was 18. I was in the early admissions summer program at Salem State College, a program that helps students with math and science before they start the fall semester. I met counselors and some great people who spoke in a positive way. They helped me see the good and positive things that I had accomplished, and the potential that was inside me. As I started believing what they saw and said, I began seeing myself in the way they were describing.

And so my journey to reframe the negative into the positive began. It was, and continues to be, a journey. I'm still on the path of seeing the best, believing the best, and speaking the best. And, when things seem negative or hopeless to me, I have to dig deep down and create a better outcome in the canvas of my imagination. I have to see the situation differently, so it can be reframed in my mind as positive. I have come to believe that there can be a positive lesson even in negative circumstances. This has taught me to have a different perspective and see negative circumstances as a temporary state, subject to change when I see it differently, speak differently and believe differently. In turn that changes my behavior and my actions, which produces the results I want.

2. Take action and move toward what you truly want.

Because I focused on what was possible and kept working and pushing, I was the first of my family to graduate from high school. It wasn't easy with English as a second language and many obstacles, but I was determined. So, although I was not the best student, I kept seeking to learn. I graduated from high school, went on to a junior college, and received my Bachelor's in Social Work. I value education and I am committed to life-long learning. I realize that, the more I learn, the more empowered I become. I want to be able to share that sense of freedom and accomplishment with others at some point, in hopes that my story will breathe life into someone else's dream.

It's not as important to know the exact destination, as to begin moving. To take action, I joined the military to help with my education, not really knowing how far I would go. Years later, I found myself as company commander of a medical unit. When you take action, God uses your experience to change your life.

3. Find great role models to learn from.

Stay around people that can show you there is something bigger, people who are going in the direction that you want to go. My first significant influence outside my family was a high school guidance counselor. He believed in me and suggested that I could go to college. He inspired me and gave me the courage to walk toward his vision until it became my own. As with many immigrants, a lot of Cape Verdeans come to the United States who have not really had the opportunity to learn the language. They come and immediately take jobs in factories to make a better life for themselves and their families. They work hard - not only provide for their families in the U.S. - but also to send money to family back in the "Old Country." Their focus is on subsistence. They work to sustain their families. So, although my mother was a real go-getter and had many dreams, she didn't have the encouragement and push that I did to continue to dream and take steps towards those dreams.

I thank God for my mother. She was my first true mentor, my role model. While she did not achieve her full potential, she did the absolute best that she could. She didn't quit. She knew there were bigger things in the world, and within the constraints of her life, she looked for new ways of getting things done.

4. Create a support system.

Find people who want the best for you and add to your life in a positive way. They become your community.

One significant part of my support system was and is the church and the positive relationships there. I met my best friend as an adult in church. She has been my biggest cheerleader who challenges me to live on purpose and enjoy the journey. I believe everyone needs a best friend who tells them the truth and accepts them without conditions. From that relationship, I now have a cadre of women who are as supportive and encouraging of my dreams as I am of theirs.

Having an intimate relationship with God is the foundation for effective support systems. We can always talk to God. He's always there. Knowing that has been a grounding point for me. There also was a college community of people who cheered me on, who nurtured, encouraged and celebrated me. These multiple systems have cradled me and aided in the journey to getting where I am today.

In order to create your own support system, define your interests and look for others who share those interests. I am interested in spirituality and the things of God, so a church community fits really well. Social work was my major, and I was interested in people and relationships. Fortunately, I found some positive groups and positive support systems to connect with. Even today, new opportunities come about through relationships with positive people, others who push me forward and challenge me to be my best.

5. Disconnect from the challenge and adversity you are facing to gain a new perspective.

Do something just for yourself. It may be reading, listening to music, or spending time in nature. Disconnecting from a problem helps us get a more objective view of it.

Going to the beach, for a walk, or to a park brings clarity and a different perspective. It provides an opportunity to ask the question, "How can I turn this adversity into a victory or into something more positive?" Refuse to stay stuck in the problem; seek a way out. There is always another way. Ask questions until you find answers.

6. Value and take good care of yourself.

When we value ourselves, other people value us. When we value ourselves, we take care of ourselves and our relationships become healthier. We have good boundaries, and we are enriched by shared positive energy and mutual regard.

We train people how to treat us. When we take care of ourselves, we show those around us that we are worthy of being taken care of. When I take care of myself, I'm a better mother. I'm the better wife. I'm a better employee. I'm a better person who can contribute more to the world and those around me. In self-care, I replenish my resources. This makes it possible for me to give more to others from a place of abundance.

One of the key facets of valuing ourselves is to find things we enjoy. It's important to know yourself and the things that bring you happiness and joy. Take time to enjoy those things without feeling guilty. For so many years, I felt guilty if I was taking time for myself, especially if I was doing something that only I enjoyed. Guilt may prompt us to do what everybody else wants, but not necessarily what we want or enjoy. Make the quality decision to enjoy today and to maximize the journey called life.

7. Never give up.

We may try a hundred things and not much will change until we try number one hundred and one. Then success happens! Had we given up at action one hundred (because we think, "I've done everything"), we would have remained in that negative place. Keep trying new things. Don't give up. Don't stop trying. Don't stop looking for solutions. Don't stop engaging. Don't quit. Right on the other side is your success, the answer you are seeking.

I learned this when I started going to school here in the U.S. At age nine, I was placed in the 4th grade. Thank God for the ESL (English as a Second Language) program, which was in Portuguese and English. That was helpful, but it ended too soon, at the end of middle school.

While everybody else was learning punctuation, grammar and a higher level of math, I was still working to add to my vocabulary- learning the difference between Tuesday and Thursday. I was learning the days of the week, numbers, and the alphabet (the things you learn in kindergarten) in the 4th grade. As an immigrant child, I was at a great disadvantage compared to others in my class. I was always in catch-up mode.

I realized very early that I had to keep on keeping on. I had to keep trying, keep doing, and keep working, if I was going to attain the things that I had heard were possible in America.

8. Give back.

As I look at a collage of pictures from a mission trip to Cape Verde, I am reminded of how very important it is to give back. Others who are struggling or facing difficulties are all around us. As dire as we may think our situation is, we don't have to look far to find someone facing a bigger challenge or in a more desperate place. Sometimes, just offering a smile or a word of encouragement can bring hope and change to someone else's outlook and brighten their day. This costs us nothing. It is worth making a difference in someone else's life even if it's in small things.

As we give back, we must be authentic and transparent. Sharing our story and journey, with compassion and insight into what is possible, is so very powerful. I remind myself of my humble beginnings and what it felt like to be that frightened, nine-year-old girl who could not communicate and had to start at the very beginning to learn how to function in a new environment. Sometimes, others see where I am now and have no idea of my story, about all the challenges, struggles, long nights, tears and sheer determination to keep going that made it all possible. By sharing our story and being authentic and transparent, we offer hope to others.

Next Success Steps

No matter what stage of life we are in or how old we are, we all face adversity in life. There is no adversity that can't be overcome. Even when the situation seems hopeless, there is a way out if we apply the steps in this chapter.

By refusing to give up, surrounding ourselves with positive role models, creating the right support system, and changing our self-talk, we can transform our lives and the situation we are facing. We can create our own joy and give back to others if we will take care of ourselves and disconnect from the adversity so we can reframe it and move towards a solution.

For this shy, timid, fearful little girl that came from a poor third-world country, there didn't seem to be a way to overcome and attain this life; however, with perseverance, faith, and the right support I was able to overcome and excel. You can do it too!

If you find yourself facing an adversity or challenge that seems bigger than you can handle, please connect with me at http://womenempoweredinternational.com/. My email address is candi@womenempoweredinternational.com. I'd love to help and support you as you navigate what may seem impossible and discover that you, too, can overcome and get to the other side faster and with more peace and intention.

About the Author

Candi Stewart serves as the Executive Pastor and co-Founder of International Family Worship Center, a thriving church in New London, CT. She and her husband of 27 years are committed to strengthening families and teaching empowered living through faith. They have four children, Tiara, Isaiah, Lenora and Joshua.

Candi holds a Master's degree in Marriage and Family Therapy and has a passion to see marriages thrive. She strives to live on purpose and help others to find their purpose and do the same. Candi enjoys mission work, traveling, movies, nature, books, and time with close friends and family.

Chapter 3

The Power of Intention: 4 Steps that Can Change Your Life

Trindalin Browning

"Your son has liver cancer," the doctor informs me. The diagnosis is hepatoblastoma, an uncommon malignant liver cancer occurring in infants and children.

But he is only 3 months old! How can this be happening to him, to us as a family, and to me as his mom? Why my baby boy? I feel so lost, heartbroken, and devastated. I have so many questions and I don't have any idea where to begin to get answers..

This news and situation changed my entire world. It really shook the foundation of who I am and everything that I thought that I was. Even before this happened, I tried to control not only my life but the lives of others around me. I refused to accept it or face the reality that it really was happening.

I found myself feeling bitter, angry, and resentful towards not only the situation but the doctors and people around me, even the ones who sincerely wanted to help. I had a very strong support system with my husband, my parents, my sister, and my other family and friends. Yet that wasn't enough for me. As I wallowed in self-pity, I would not allow the people closest to me to help me as they wanted (and I truly needed). Instead I pushed them away, and nursed my anger and fear.

Looking back, I realize the person I resented the most was my husband. I felt as if he should have been there more for both me and our son. When the diagnosis was made, my husband traveled a lot. He wasn't there throughout the beginning stages with all the tests, appointments, and efforts to gather information and determine the right treatment. During the chemotherapy treatments and surgeries, he was absent more than I wanted. While I knew intellectually he needed to work to provide for us, the resentment toward him continued to grow. How could he have left me and our son when we needed him the most?

I was fooling myself into thinking that I was okay. Yet I was just masking my feelings, and the simplest things would set me off. My husband could leave a pair of shoes in the floor or crumbs on the table and I boiled with anger. This caused a real wedge between us. My husband kept asking "What's wrong? Why are you acting like that?" I even wondered, "Why am I so angry with him?" I couldn't verbalize my feelings, so he was left confused and unable to respond.

I harbored this resentment for fifteen years.

Slowly, I began to realize that, for my own sake and for my son and family, I had to somehow heal and move beyond the anger. I had allowed my son's medical situation and the daily stresses and commitments to not only overwhelm me but toss me around until I was battered and bleeding.

I eventually started counseling and realized the way I was living was unhealthy for me and everyone I loved. I could no longer continue on the destructive path I was on and I needed to be honest about what and how I was feeling. I can't say the change was immediate. I had gotten used to living with this chip on my shoulder so I gave up my grudges reluctantly. It was difficult to look in the mirror and be honest about my behavior; however, taking that look was necessary. It was difficult realizing I was locked in a self-destructive place because of MY thoughts and actions. It was even more difficult to see a way out. So, I did what my therapist suggested.

It wasn't until I started writing and journaling that I began to identify the triggers and to see the true causes of my behavior. I began to realize how much damage had been caused by my constant anger and bitterness over what life had dealt me. I had made this situation all about me. Ultimately it was about my son and my being the mom that I needed to be to help him get better. Journaling allowed me to be honest with myself and accept my current circumstance. It allowed me to see beyond that situation to envision - and ultimately create - a real, honest and effective way to become free.

The healing journey to living intentionally begins

I made a big decision: I would live my life with intention instead of being tossed back and forth with whatever came my way. I now have a clear purpose and meaning in my life.

Being intentional meant I chose to make each day meaningful and do what I could to improve my life and current state of being. I began to write and plan out my day and that helped me create my pathway to forgiveness.

I didn't reveal my deepest thoughts to my husband until just a few years ago. When I finally shared my true feelings, I was able to release the rage, bitterness and anger. Looking back I realized that all those days, months, and years when I felt so alone in this crisis, much of my pain was self-inflicted.

That was fifteen years of time when we could have supported, cared, and nurtured each other and our relationship, time that we can never get back. As I let go of all the bitterness, pain and resentment and the healing journey began, my husband and I found our way to forgiveness. Despite the time that was lost to us, our marriage and our friendship are stronger because there is nothing hidden, no wedge between us. By accepting the reality of our situation, addressing the issues, and moving forward with intention, my life and our relationship changed.

I followed four key steps to get back on the right path and move forward powerfully and with intention.

The Power of Intention: Four Steps that Can Change Your Life

1. Be honest about who you are as a person and what makes you happy.

Set aside the thoughts of who you are as a mom, wife, sister, daughter, friend, or anything else.

Take a close look and be honest about who you are as a person. This will require soul searching and quiet time in your own space. For me journaling, prayer, and meditation were the key tools for discovering what truly makes me happy.

Most of us have given very little or no thought to what really makes us happy. We are too busy taking care of everyone else to even realize that our own happiness matters. It may be taking walks on the beach, going to the park, or enjoying a good book.

When we don't take time to know what truly makes us happy, our lives can get caught up in what society or others say we should do or be. This can be the never-ending hamster wheel of "coulda, woulda, shouldas," leading us to beat ourselves up because we are living our lives according to someone else's standards or what they say our lives should be.

Once we start realizing who we truly are, we discover that we don't have to do or be what others expect to be accepted. Those who genuinely love us will accept us for who we truly are and will want only the best for us.

2. Don't be afraid of where you are. Accept things as they truly are.

Stop allowing the fear of the unknown – or even the known – to stop you. Fear can stop us from doing, becoming, and living our best life. The acronym FEAR stands for "false evidence appearing real." Just because it feels real, does not mean it truly is.

Sometimes, we are not clear within ourselves about what we really want and desire. We only know we want something different from what we have now.

We can hide behind the excuse of "Since I can't figure it out and since I can't see or touch it, it's not a tangible thing. I'm just not going to do anything about it." To have a different life, we must move past that. We must first accept life as it is right now and then decide this is not where I am going to stay. When we are sick and tired of where we are and the circumstances we are in, we are ready to take action to create something different for ourselves.

That may involve moving to a different location, changing your circle of friends, or enrolling in a course or program, as a few examples.

3. Address the issue so you can move on.

Whatever the problem or issue is, your life will be much better once it's addressed. It may be hard to do this, but there are rewards on the other side. When we carry issues around, never dealing with them, life becomes miserable and much more difficult. Whatever the issue or challenge is, it won't get better with time; it will only get worse.

Here is a real life example.

I am afraid to swim. I have a real fear of water. I wouldn't even take a shower and wash my hair in the shower, because I was afraid that water would get in my face. I was at the water park with my youngest son who was six at the time. He wanted to get on the rafter (inner tube). My oldest son and my nephew refused to take him on the ride. So, fighting my fears of water, I decided to do it. I'm 5' 2", so the water probably came to my chest.

As I got on the rafter, it flipped over. I found myself fully submerged in water and panicked. I am kicking and screaming in sheer terror. I hear a man's voice saying, "Ma'am, just stand up." So I stood up. I could breathe! I had no idea I was in only a few feet of water. I gathered myself and thought, "I'm good, I'm good."

Being submerged was one of the worst things I could ever imagine. But once I stood up, gathered myself, and took a couple of deep breaths, I realized I didn't die, I'm still living and I was going to be okay.

We think that if we deal with the issue, it's going to kill us. We will likely not make it out alive. But that's not the case. Most of the time, the thing that we're most afraid of never happens.

We may go under, but we'll come back up. We have to take a couple of deep breaths to get our footing back and may be knocked down, but it won't kill us. If anything, it will make us better and stronger. Now I can submerge my face in the water. I still don't swim yet, but I'm not afraid of water like I was before.

4. Accept whatever the outcome is: good, bad, or indifferent.

Most of the time, the outcome will not be nearly as bad as we think that it will. So, accept it. Even if the outcome is far from what you want, you've done your part to do what's right. Everybody will not always agree with you. Accept that as a part of life. Embrace those who love you and hold them close.

Choose to accept the outcome (whether it is good or bad) and move on from there.

Next Success Steps

Living with intention is the catalyst to get us to where we need to be and where we want to go in life. When we have no purpose or anchor, we are tossed in the wind, reacting to whatever happens each day and being battered in the process. We are swayed by what others think, say, or expect, paying no attention to what we truly want and need to have a happy life.

Do you want to live with intent, embrace life, and view each day as a gift? Know what makes you happy and what you want. Accept the reality of what you are facing. Muster the courage to address and change the situation. And be willing to accept the outcome.

Are you in a life situation right now where you can't see your way out? Are you holding on to fear, anger or resentment and don't know what to do next to make your life better? Let's set a time to talk about your biggest challenge and the next few steps you can take to move forward. Connect with me at Women Empowered International. My email address is trindalin@womenempoweredinternational.com.

About the Author

Trindalin Browning is known as "the quiet storm" for her ability to not only influence others but pull out the best in people. She loves working with women to help them identify, accept and realize their potential; learn about who they truly are; inspire them to truly love themselves; and push them to walk in their greatness. She hopes to one day see a world where all women can walk in who they truly are without any inhibitions or hang-ups.

Serving as a senior account manager for Polay Clark & Company, she holds a Bachelor's degree in Business Management and also is certified in QuickBooks and Xero Accounting software.

Trindalin is mom to two amazing children and a loving wife who spends her spare time reading, volunteering at her church, spending time with friends and family, and helping women learn how to live with intention so they can have a full and happy life.

You can learn more about Trindalinís mission to help women at Women Empowered International (WomeneEmpoweredInternational.com). Her email address is trindalin@womenempoweredinternational. com.

Chapter 4

Beyond the Diagnosis: 8 Steps to Move Forward with Grace and Ease

Tracie Randolph

"You have breast cancer. The results from the biopsies were positive," the doctor shares with not much emotion. As I sit in the chair, I feel nothing but numbness and shock.

I sought medical help when I felt a sharp pain in my right breast. I didn't think too much of it, but I decided to err on the side of caution and go to the doctor. My doctor didn't really seem concerned. He sent me for a mammogram as a precaution.

The mammogram revealed two different tumors in my right breast, both very small. Throughout that whole process I thought, "I am forty-two and pretty healthy. I don't smoke, and I don't drink much. There's no history of breast cancer in my family. This is just routine."

I had so completely convinced myself that everything was okay that I came here alone today.

I am in shock, with no one in the room to support and care for me in that moment. I realize I have to deal with this diagnosis and figure out what to do next.

My journey forward

As I was leaving the doctor's office, I received a call from my cousin Tamara, who is a very spiritual person. It amazed me that she decided to check on me at the very moment when I needed it most. As I shared the news of the diagnosis, she gave me a very valuable piece of advice in one word: "Relax." When we think about relaxation, we naturally let go and breathe.

I was still in shock but decided to hold on to my faith, move forward, and find joy in the people and things that make me happy. My son, the light of my life, kept me anchored. I focused on his life and how much I wanted and needed to continue to be there for him. This kept me grounded and helped me deal with every doctor's visit, surgery, and treatment. I was surrounded by a very supportive family and group of friends who, in even the simplest conversations, helped me stay positive. I also decided that I would combat cancer by learning more about stress management, food, and nutrition to help prepare my body to fight. In my pursuit to learn more about keeping my own body, mind, and spirit healthy, I unearthed an intense passion for supporting other people who find themselves faced with a serious medical diagnosis.

Along the way, I also discovered eight steps to move forward with grace and ease after a serious medical diagnosis.

Eight Steps for Moving Forward with Grace

1. Manage your stress through breath.

When you receive difficult news or have a life-changing experience, your body will react with an immediate stress response. **Take a deep breath.** And then another. Repeat. Just stop for a moment to de-stress and allow time to absorb what has happened. Try to relax and breathe before making any decisions, going into research mode, or telling family.

In and of itself, breathing brings some relief from stress. It provides us with room to think more clearly, move forward, and deal with all the things that need to be taken care of (doctor appointments, medical tests, treatments, and family obligations). Make time for a few minutes of conscious breathing throughout each day.

2. Adopt a positive attitude.

A lot of stress and sickness can come from how we think. If your mind is telling you that you're sick and can't get through it, that will be true for you. As we train ourselves or reframe our thinking and mindset to the positive, we begin to know that we **can** make it to the other side of this diagnosis and treatment. Cultivating a positive attitude helps significantly with our healing.

Focusing on the negative increases our stress levels. Stress is a big part of what breaks our bodies down, both psychologically and physically. Cortisol, which is secreted as a part of the stress response, suppresses the immune system and can definitely play a part in your body's ability to heal.

3. Pray.

Connect (or reconnect) with God or your higher power. Nothing happens by accident.

My cousin calling at just that moment was divinely ordered. We are both spiritually minded and naturally connected in that way, and her support was God sent at just the right moment.

We find strength in a higher power and can lean on that higher power to know we can get through any disease or challenge we are going through. We realize we are indeed strong and not alone as we work through what lies ahead.

I'm a person who prays a lot; in fact, it is a habit. So, it was very natural for me to pray - not only about the situation - but also about what to do with the information from the doctors as well as the decisions I had to make. I asked for strength to deal with each day as it came and for clarity to make the right choices.

4. Focus on the people and things you love.

My son was six at the time of my diagnosis. Focusing on him and understanding that he needed me as his mom were keys to my ability to heal and keep moving forward. Death was not an option! This little person needed me in his life. And I wanted to be there for him. So I focused on him more than I focused on myself. Shifting my focus helped me get through the situation.

What you truly love can be anyone or anything. It could be your parents, your children, or your pet, or it may be doing the things that you love. Taking walks or going for bike rides, listening to music, or watching movies. Do the things that speak to your heart and bring you joy (as long as your doctor approves while you are healing and recovering).

Look for what is good in the world - the people, nature, the things that make you laugh or smile, and whatever brings you pure happiness.

5. Develop affirmations.

Using affirmations is also a powerful tool. Tell yourself that it will be okay. Develop affirmations as you work on your positive attitude. Try reframing any negative thoughts to positive thoughts. For example, if you are thinking, "I feel so tired and weak today," switch that to "I'm healthy and strong and getting better every day." Be kind and loving to yourself as you go through this healing and treatment journey.

6. Eat well.

We all know that what we are putting in the body as food affects our physical health. Having a healthy diet can cleanse the body from the inside, as well.

Anyone with cancer should take a close look at lifestyle and identify ways to help the body rebuild. The way to do that is to focus on pure foods, such as whole fruits and vegetables and good grains that can be easily digested. Of course, drinking a lot of water is a part of that as well.

Something that a nutritionist told me years ago is very wise advice: if you don't understand the ingredients on the label or don't know what it is, it's probably not good for you. Focus on the intake of whole foods throughout this process. Avoid preservatives and chemicals in your food sources. Minimizing sugar intake is also believed to be beneficial.

For those who have no idea where to start with implementing a healthy diet, a nutritionist or dietician can help you create a meal plan that works with your lifestyle. Health coaches can help with lifestyle changes and making healthy eating habits that are sustained.

7. Incorporate movement and exercise.

Along with eating right, we also need to find ways to incorporate movement and exercise into our days. Movement has definitely been proven to help people mitigate the risk of disease or assist in the healing process.

The web site Physical-Fitess-Exercises.com reflects the following startling statistics:

> Men are 45% more likely to die from cancer if they live a sedentary (inactive) lifestyle and women who are inactive are 28% more likely to die from cancer than those who exercise regularly. Men who are inactive have a 52% higher chance of dying from heart disease and women have a 28% higher risk of death from heart disease if they are inactive.
>
> Regular moderate exercise or other physical activity in addition to a balanced diet can reduce the risk of developing diabetes by 50-60%; blood pressure can be decreased by approximately 75% by exercising regularly. Physical activity reduces the risk of heart disease by 27-41%.

It doesn't have to be rigorous exercise; any form of movement works well. Walking is a great choice, especially for those who have been sedentary. Start by walking around the block first. As you gain strength, walk further. Just being outside helps lift your spirits. Getting some form of exercise at least 20 minutes 4 to 5 times per week can make the world of difference to your health and well-being.

When my mom had a heart attack, she needed to lose weight as an important part of regaining her health. She started walking, a little bit at a time, without doing any other exercise. She also changed her diet. And with these choices she has increased energy, decreased her cholesterol and blood pressure, reversed her hypertension, lost weight, and achieved a new sense of confidence.

8. Understand our connection to the environment.

Everything in our world is connected. For example, how we eat and what times we eat are definitely connected to the environment. The warmer hours of our day are when we should eat our biggest meal. Doctors tell people, "Don't eat after 8:00 p.m." There's real meaning behind that, because our body doesn't digest the food as easily as it would earlier during the day. Lunch should be our largest meal, because it's when both the Earth and our body are heated more. When your body is heated more, it allows the body to digest a lot more. Digestion is a key process that allows the body to get rid of toxins. Connecting to the environment is important for proper digestion and proper healing.

Make your home environment healthier. Remove household toxins by using safer cleaning supplies. A wide variety of safer cleaning products are available. We have access to everything from laundry detergent to bathroom cleaners and solutions for cleaning floors and windows.

Safer products are out there to give us options. Look for more natural supplements, as well. When choosing a supplement, use the rule of thumb you use with food - if you don't know the ingredient, it's probably not good for you.

Next Success Steps

Know that the word "cancer" is not a death sentence. There **is** life after you learn of your diagnosis. You can get through it and live a full and happy life.

As you have learned in this chapter, there are ways to make our bodies, minds, and spirits stronger and healthier as we're dealing with cancer and cancer treatment. Mindful breathing, eating properly, focusing on those we love, prayer and meditation, and movement all help us stay grounded and moving forward, especially on the "down" days.

By taking good care of ourselves while we are going through the treatments and healing, we can move through the process with more ease, knowing we are not in this situation alone.

Are you a woman facing a life-changing diagnosis and wondering how you'll survive it? Are you struggling to make sense of it all so you can put your life back together?

Let's connect and have a conversation about your challenges and what you can do right now to move forward. Just email me at tracie@womenempoweredinternational. com.

About the Author

Tracie Randolph has had a successful corporate career for over 20 years and understands the stress in balancing work and family, which has given Tracie a perspective on the need for holistic wellness. Her passion for health, nutrition and overall holistic wellness was born from her own struggle to regain her health after a cancer diagnosis. She perceives having cancer as one of the most amazing things that happened in her life; leading her to a life of purpose to point others towards optimal health.

As a health coach, Tracie understands how intimately challenging, yet how satisfying it can be to make sustainable lifestyle changes that have a lasting impact on one's overall well-being. She is a supportive mentor who motivates people to cultivate positive health choices.

Tracie received her training and certification as a health coach from Health Coach Institute, a program accredited by the International Coach Federation. Tracie has her mentoring certification and will receive her life coaching certification in May 2018 from Women Empowered's Breakthrough University.

Tracie enjoys a pure zest for life and wants to help people get true joy and fulfillment out of this one life that they have to live. Being the mother of a beautiful, smart, inquisitive and loving son is a major part of her life's joy. Seeing the world through his eyes gives her a fresh perspective that allows her to approach life with curiosity and care. She strives to live a joy-filled life and her mission is to support others to do the same.

If you are looking to understand how you can move on and be at your best and most optimal health after a medical diagnosis, if you want to approach life and be proactive about your wellness, if you are struggling with stress and want to mitigate the stress to avoid other complications, or if you just want to understand more about holistic wellness, contact her at tracie@womenempoweredinternational.com.

Chapter 5

Building Resiliency:
5 Proven Steps to Overcome Adversity with Grace, Faith and Intent

Shema Stroud

I smile to myself as I sink down into the salon chair. I am excited to treat myself to a new hair style. I've been here for manicures and pedicures and received good service. Why not let them do my hair?

The stylist is a beautiful woman, high-spirited and friendly. We're both in our early thirties and the conversation flows freely and easily. She takes my hair out of a ponytail style bun as I talk away. Suddenly, I notice she's become very quiet.

A few seconds later, she says, "Oh my God. I need to take you into the back room for a minute." "Okay," I reply, as I get up to follow her. We walk into the back room and she begins to tell me there's a problem with my hair. "If you don't mind, would you allow me to pray with you and pray over your hair?"

I had noticed recently that some hair had fallen out in a few areas, so I assume that she may have seen a few bald spots and is overreacting. I allow her to pray for me.

When she finishes, she asks me to turn towards the mirror so she can explain to me what she's seen. When I look in the mirror, I'm stunned to see I have no hair on my head. My hair is gone!

She is standing there with the ponytail extension in her hand. All of the hair that's fallen out is attached to the bun. Tears are running down the stylist's face and now I'm horrified! I am literally in shock.

I don't know what to do at this point. This is not one or two bald spots. 90 percent of my hair is completely gone. The only thing to do is to cut what remains, so she snips those few pieces that are still connected.

My head looks like that of a dog with mange; one who has lost most of its hair and only skin is showing with small patches of fuzz here and there. I don't know what to do. I'm freaking out, crying hysterically.

I am 35 minutes away from home. I call my mother; but can't articulate what has happened with any understandable words. Somehow I make it home, knowing Mom is worried that I'm driving alone in this emotional state. Thank God I made it safely!

Without an explanation for what is happening, I plunge into depression and melt into a ball of nothing. That's the way it felt. There is no fight and no energy left inside me. I don't know what to do with this. I don't want to do anything. I don't want to talk to anyone. I don't want to see anyone. So I go to bed, planning to stay there indefinitely.

The very next morning, Mom wakes me up as if nothing has happened. She's standing at my doorway. I feel her watching me. I turn to her and she says, "Are you ready?" "Ready for what?" I reply. "We have to go get you hair. We're going to get you wigs, and we're going to figure this out. So get dressed, and we're out of here."

That was my first moment – my initial step towards accepting what had happened to me. I literally do not have any hair. It's Saturday. I have to figure out what I'm going to do between Saturday morning and Monday morning – when I have to go back to work.

Resiliency: The Journey Begins

This is where my journey to build resiliency began.

There are so many things that society uses to define us as women. At the age of 33, and in this situation, I thought that my hair was on the top of that list. My self-esteem was gone. I felt I was less of a woman and that I had less than other women.

The pain, hurt, and depression that come from a major setback can make us feel as if it is the end. Adversity can beat us down so much that we begin to feel less than we are and believe there is no coming back. I want women to understand that this is **not** true. There is always an opportunity to recover from any setback you encounter.

From my personal adversities, I have learned the five proven steps for dealing with a life-changing situation and becoming more resilient with grace, faith, and intent.

Five Proven Steps for Dealing with a Life-Changing Situation and Becoming Stronger and More Resilient

1. Accept the situation.

Sometimes what we are experiencing seems surreal-beyond belief that it is actually happening. I am looking in the mirror and I don't fully comprehend what the stylist is telling me, "You have lost all your hair." I saw it and I still couldn't believe it.

We have to accept what is, the reality of the situation, so that we can move on to the next thing. We may be devastated by what has happened, but it didn't kill us. So, what do we need to do next?

A big part of "accepting it" for me was to dig into it, to try to understand. Was it something I did? Was it part of an illness over which I had no control? I looked at it straight on and from every angle.

Is there a way to fix it? Do I need to take medicine? Is there some form of treatment? I asked a ton of questions, but I didn't always like the answers that I was given. The condition that attacked me affected the hair on every part of my body; all my hair was falling out and all at the same time. It had a name - alopecia universalis – but the prognosis was uncertain. I was told it would not likely go away, so I would have to learn to live with it…at least for a while.

Accepting the situation requires more than inquiry and examination. You must also find a new way to be in the new situation. For me, that meant I needed things to seem as "normal" as possible. I needed to act as if everything was the same, to behave as much as possible as the Shema that I'd known for more than 30 years. When I went to look for a new wig, hair piece or accessory, I wanted it to look as much as possible like the hairstyles I'd worn in the past. I wasn't looking to change anything. At that point, I just wanted to be normal for a minute. I wanted my world not to be upside-down.

You may need to allow for more sleep or time alone. Honor your own needs. During this time of acceptance, look for the courage to move forward with life as you now know it. There may well be stumbling but not stopping. Life will continue and you will also, just in a different way. This setback becomes a part of your story but it doesn't define you.

2. Release the anger.

When we're going through adversity, there are a couple of places it can take you, including further down into depression or into complete anger.

I became extremely angry. I was brooding over questions that have no answers. I attributed motives and thoughts to people before they even had a chance to engage or respond. I scourged myself with doubts. I imagined a lonely future, rejected by everyone. I was spiraling downward with increasingly dismal answers to the sorts of questions that plague us during adversity:

- Why did this happen to me?
- What did I do to deserve this?
- What do I do with this?
- How are others going to perceive me and this situation?

I wallowed in self-pity. I was a young woman who wanted to have a relationship with a decent guy. I wanted to go on dates and have a normal life. How could I have a normal life when I didn't have a normal situation?

When your mind is spinning with questions that have no answers and you are looking for someone or something to blame, it is easy to become angry. To release anger, we first need to face it. Allow ourselves to grieve, to forgive. The reality for me was that I had nothing or no one to blame. My body literally attacked itself. How do I fight an unseen adversary? I admitted my anger, and began to develop ways to move past it.

I turned to God to help me release the anger and hurt. I prayed for strength and God's guidance to move forward. My faith is my source of strength. Your source of strength may differ from mine, but the key to moving forward is to find it wherever you can.

3. Find the right people and environment to fight our way back.

There are times when our own strength is depleted. In these times, our faith may falter. In these moments, we gather strength from others.

My mom played a key role in this process. She was the one that showed up. She made me get out of bed and take that first critical step toward reclaiming my life. She was a calming force. She had the ability to instill her strength in me, not only in this situation but in so many others.

My mother and I have an amazing relationship. Not everyone has that. This important unwavering support doesn't have to come from family members. Find that person, those people, or those environments that give you strength and affirm you. When we have a support system, we can lean on it until we are able to stand on our own. Don't ever be afraid to lean on your supporters to find your way back. They are all part of your strength.

4. Define our new "normal."

I finally came to understand that I had to redefine my new "normal." I am a dark-haired woman. My black hair had always been pretty healthy, medium-length, and very thin and fine. While at first I wanted so much to look like my original self, I began to wonder if there was another way.

I began experimenting with wigs and hair extensions. I bought different colors and textures. Then, I tried a variety of lengths. None of this changed who I was inside; it just changed the look. With each new experiment, I grew braver.

People's reactions both surprised and affirmed me. They weren't saying, "Oh, what are you doing with your hair?" or "Why are you changing your hair so often?" or "You don't look like yourself." What I heard was

- That's cute.
- That's different.
- You're so brave; you'll try anything.
- You look good in anything.

Combined with my own courage, it just took a few comments from other people to jump out there and try something new that made me say, "You know what? I can own this. My style doesn't have to be cookie-cutter. It can be whatever I want it to be." Okay, I lost the hair. I spent quite a few years trying to figure out why before embracing it and making it what I wanted. I finally realized I can be brave and take chances; and, in doing so, inspire others to do the same. In turn, I can inspire myself to take the next chance, and the next. You may not decide when and how you are thrust into crisis, but you can definitely decide how you will come out of it.

5. Embrace our new future.

Know that the pain, hurt, and adversity are what fuels us to better ourselves, to take the next step, to do more, and to give back in a more powerful way.

We can leverage this setback, this new challenge, to change our future. We can turn it into a positive and add it to a growing kit of tools used to help us overcome and become a better version of ourselves. In essence, this experience can be a stepping stone for building a new future that can be filled with joy and peace.

Closing thoughts

When faced with adversity, we each must accept what is. We must explore our options and take positive action. We must accept help and surround ourselves with the right people and environment. We must recognize our anger and grief and release it. We must define our new normal bravely and include some fun if we can.

We also need to be gentle with ourselves as we may need to repeat these steps as we move through the adversity. As we give ourselves permission to feel while we move through each step, we can embrace our new future and, as they say, "lather, rinse and repeat"!

Next Success Steps

My greatest desire is to provide hope to other women. There's no storybook way of putting it. There are no rules or regulations in experimenting and exploring who we are and what we can do when faced with adversity.

As I think about this experience and overcoming it, I realize that I've always been a kid at heart. I still am. I'm still that kid who stands on the dresser with the pillow case super hero cape tied around my neck – hoping to make it to the bed when I take this large leap. Even at my age, I'm still taking those leaps. I'm still doing kid things. What I've learned about being a kid at heart is that you can do anything.

Think about it. There is no greater example of resiliency than a child. They bounce back from so many things. It's not until we are older that we build a wall of resistance. We develop the self-limiting belief that this is all there is for us in life and allow our adversity to define who we are. It absolutely does **not** define us.

Consider those instances or situations in your life that created doubt or were confusing or painful, when you thought - this is the end. I don't know how I can get over this. Then consider how you overcame it. You did it! The same strength that brought you through those times is available as you need it moving forward.

Are you a woman in the midst of adversity right now? Or maybe there was a situation in the past, perhaps even years ago, that has never been addressed or healed. If you are ready to find help to accept and release it so you can create the "new normal" for your life, let's talk! Email me at shema@womenempoweredinternational.com.

About the Author

Shema Stroud is a life coach, mentor and author whose passion is to serve others. She holds a B. S. in Accounting from Saint Leo University of Florida, a Lean Six Sigma Certification from Villanova University, and a Mentor Certification from Women Empowered. She has worked in a range of fields, including Education, Finance, and Telecommunications. In addition, she owns a beauty business called "Smile Gorgeously."

Shema is as natural storyteller who has always loved sharing life's experiences with others in vivid and living color. She is a true kid at heart, tapping into boundless wonder and fearless exploration. A New Jersey girl, Shema was born in Paterson, and raised in Ridgewood where she currently resides. She comes from a large family, and revels in her family and heritage. She has traveled throughout the U.S. and numerous international destinations, including Italy, Greece, and Turkey.

Shema's mission is to live a life filled with joyful experiences, amazing travels and purposeful interactions according to God's promises. She encourages her clients to manifest the light of God's love in their own lives and pay it forward in service to others.

Shema is also an active member of her church, a number of community organizations and the Women Empowered organization which she credits with setting her on the path to living her life on purpose and with full intent.

For more information on living your life on purpose, please visit WomenEmpoweredInternational.com.

For questions or conversations with Shema, feel free to contact her via email: shema@womenempoweredinternational.com or connect with her on LinkedIn (www.LinkedIn/in/shemastroud).

Chapter 6

From Dream to Reality: 11 Steps for Creating Your Path to Success

Melissa Simmons

"Hand in your resignation," the state monitor across the desk from me blurts out. "You have an hour to collect your things and leave the building."

As a key leader in a school district that was run by the state, I witnessed the recent dismissal of the previous superintendent. I know that the monitor is politically motivated to push the agenda of the board. Yet, just last Friday, the interim superintendent told me he was recommending me for a contract (and I technically already had tenure). Apparently, something had changed over the weekend!

I ask, "Why? Why would I do that?" She replies, "We know that you didn't do anything wrong, and you've been doing a good job. The board doesn't feel that you have their agenda in mind." My loyalty to the superintendent who had just been dismissed, the man who hired me, is now working against me. I try hard to accept her words. She continues, "They will attack your name and reputation if you don't give me your resignation. You will find yourself not only without a job, but with your name tarnished."

I had been in the field of state education for almost twenty years. Her words sting; indeed, they take my breath away. I am an excellent administrator who has done everything right. While I had studied accounting and auditing, I learned quickly that my real passion lies in working with people and helping them move forward. I am a great leader who is making changes in the workplace. I push and am a voice for my managers and teams. I encourage them to advance toward their dreams and career aspirations.

Now, my career lays in the hands of one person who wasn't interested in my being part of the senior team. In that political work environment, I was not the person they wanted in that role. I did too many things the right way and that wasn't the way they wanted it. While I know I did nothing to deserve this, I also know I can't fight the political "machine." But I **could** fight for my name. So, I decide to walk away from the situation, my job and maybe my career.

I feel a profound emptiness as I go back to my office and look around to see what I want to take. The only things that have any real meaning at that moment are my nameplate and the pictures of my family on my desk. Nothing else in that office matters now.

I somehow drive myself home, feeling very empty and lost. I feel like a failure to my staff. They see me as an advocate for their success and look to me for "protection" from the political environment. Now, they are on their own to deal with whatever happens next. Since I work for one of the largest districts in the state, I feel like a failure on a public level as well.

How do I go home and tell my daughter and my son, "Mommy got fired"? How do I call my husband and let him know, "Honey, I don't have a job and I honestly don't know what's going to happen in the next couple months"? I had worked so hard in my career to provide for my family, and now there was nothing to show for it. My efforts and the recognition I had received for my accomplishments have come to nothing. Without a financial net, I feel like a failure to all the people I love. Staring at my nameplate, I remember this verse from Genesis 12:

"Now the Lord said to Abram, 'Go forth from your country, And from your relatives And from your father's house, To the land which I will show you; 2 And I will make you a great nation, And I will bless you, And make your name great, And so you shall be a blessing, 3 And I will bless those who bless you, And the one who curses you I will curse. And in you all the families of the earth will be blessed.'"

This verse reminds me that I now need to look up to God who is the One who makes each of our names great.

The Journey to Creating a Path to Success Begins!

Up to this very moment, I thought that I was living my life intentionally. Now I see this was not true; I was far off that path. The position I had did not fill my soul or fulfill my calling to help others in a powerful way. One close colleague had warned me, "Be careful, and prepare for the next step." Because I didn't heed that advice, I had no plan in place for my next step.

It was not easy to regroup. I thought that I would go on a few interviews, land a new job and everything would be okay. As the months went on, I knew I had to take control of my own life and career.

My mentor called and I shared what happened. I've never forgotten her words, "Don't worry. Resigning was probably your opportunity." This was the key to the most profound lessons of my life.

Despite how it may look or feel, failure is not failure if you use it as an opportunity on your path forward. At that moment, I also realized that I had a career but *not* a calling. A calling is when you are doing what you have been born to do and have a passion to do. I did business administration well, and it will serve me well in the future, but it is not my calling.

Now, I had to do for myself what I helped my managers and teams do for so many years. At the moment of what I perceived to be my most profound failure, I had to create a new opportunity and find my path forward. I started exploring what I wanted to do. From the outside, others saw me as a success. I had a good job, making what most people would consider to be good money. But I had not tapped into my passion.

I also wanted to be the master of my own path. I wanted to be in a position where regardless of the work I'm doing or where I am doing it, I have more power over my life than anyone else.

At that time, I wrote a book that I'd wanted to write for years. My husband and I offered advice about how to have a good marriage. When we spoke to groups, we were advocates and coaches for marriage. I made another decision: I wanted to do more than that.

One of the things that I love to do is mentor women. I learned from being an executive in the marketplace that there are very few women at the top; and even fewer minority women with whom you can collaborate to continue your growth and development for advancement. A woman in an executive role without a business mentor has no one to turn to after a hard meeting in the boardroom. They don't have someone more seasoned to explore ideas with or to advise them about practical steps as a woman leader. I truly want to be an advocate and sounding board for other women in this situation, the person they call to say, "I'm about to make a decision. Can you help me think this through?" or "This is what I'm thinking. What are your thoughts and ideas?"

From this experience, eleven steps emerged that anyone looking to create their path forward can follow to find the success they want. This process is the exact blueprint that guides me and serves as the framework for my clients.

11 Steps for Creating Your Path to Success

1. Decide *for yourself.*

So often, I find myself doing things for others, advising them on making the right decision and then helping them to make it happen. It's easy to get caught up in playing the hero. For some of us, we are so busy doing for others that we put our own needs and dreams aside.

When we start on our personal journey, we have to first make the crucial decision to do this **for ourselves**. Putting ourselves first is a hard decision for most women, because we're so accustomed to helping others. Many of us struggle when we take time for ourselves. Without that decision to "make time for what's important to me," we can't be who we need to be for everyone else in the world.

2. Commit.

The journey of exploration to find out what you want and to go after it requires a commitment of both time and finances. As a business person, I realize - if you want a return and if you want to increase your revenue - you have to invest. Investments will yield the return we're looking for, if we make them wisely.

Too often, as women, we do not make investments in ourselves. We invest in our children. We invest in our husbands. We invest in our family members. Yet, we fail to invest time and money in ourselves.

How many of us didn't finish the academic program we started? We put that Master's degree on the back burner. We didn't take that certification class or attend a conference we knew would benefit us. Neglecting our dreams happens because we make other commitments first, leaving no room for the commitment to ourselves.

As a wife and the mother of three children, I understand the sacrifices we make; however, there comes a time when we must include ourselves in the plan. We can't keep deferring our hopes and dreams, and expect our lives to change. My *'aha moment'* came when my son asked me during a college visit, "Why didn't you get your masters, Mom?" I replied to him saying, "I made a decision to be a wife and mom." Yet, although I did make that choice, a nagging question lingered. "What's stopping me now?"

Currently, my motto is "Just do it" with another key component added - "because later is still getting later." We often decide to postpone doing what we want. Then,

1, 2, 10, 15, 20 years may go by and we find ourselves in the same place.

Committing requires some level of sacrifice. It may not be easy. We will likely have to give up some things along the way and reallocate funds, time, and energy to move forward on this new path.

3. Learn from the past before moving forward.

We tend to focus on the question "Where do I go from here?" But first, we need to answer the question, "How did I get here?" When we look closely at the past with the intention to learn from it, we can see both the progress and the stumbles we made. We see the obstacles that were in our path that may have diverted us to where we are now. We can use those lessons to help guide us regarding what we need to do differently going forward.

4. Explore your options.

Having learned from our past (the good, bad, and ugly), we can now explore where we want to go next. A great first step is to define our values. What is important?

Assessing our talents, skills, and experience is the next step. Some of our greatest talents may lie dormant as we focus on taking care of others first.

Identify the skills and abilities you are good at and enjoy doing. Perhaps it's communicating and talking to people. Maybe it's writing. It could be speaking. We might re-discover activities from the past that we loved and gave up for various reasons. Within these discoveries, you may find a new passion or discover a new vocation. Enrich your life with options you never considered. Contemplate trying something new. For example, I learned that I was a musical and movie script writer. My wild imagination that my mom and sisters considered to be "overly dramatic" has served me well as an adult.

Learn about yourself and get to know yourself, perhaps for the very first time. Identify your core beliefs – those principles that capture the essence of who you are. Faithful, leader, family-centered, trustworthy, creative and artistic are just a few of my core beliefs. As I began writing them out, my core beliefs began to guide my decision making and serve as a barometer of what I would and would not do. My beliefs provided focus and direction as I began to identify steps towards my success.

5. See the good in yourself and celebrate it.

Not only do we not realize our hidden gifts and talents, we have a tough time acknowledging our accomplishments and seeing the good inside us. We are often very skilled at encouraging other people, but we have a hard time promoting ourselves. We see the good in someone else, but we have difficulty seeing the good in ourselves. Every time we receive a compliment or acknowledgment, we should celebrate ourselves! Own it! Not in an arrogant fashion, but as a humble acceptance that you are good at being you!

6. Uncover the courage to move forward with what you are called to do.

I distinctly remember returning to the workplace after I lost my job. Going back into the field, standing in front of new Boards of Education, and trying to get another position required courage. It took strength to walk into every interview. I had to have grit to stand in front of people and let them know that I was the person they needed to hire. I remember one particular board that interviewed me. They asked me why they should hire me. I had to figure out why I was good enough for them, when I clearly wasn't the right person for my last position. It took real courage to work through that and keep going. As we begin to believe in ourselves, we become braver and stronger.

Another example of real courage happened after I was hired by a board. I worked hard to prove to my board and superintendent that I was a good, if not an excellent, administrator. I held my tongue when one board member felt it was his role to speak disrespectfully and to disparage and demean me. He referred to me as "Aunt Jemima" to my superintendent and used ugly references when speaking about me to other board members. I wanted my contract renewed, but not at the cost of my own core beliefs and self-respect. Finally, I gathered my courage and informed him in front of the rest of the board that I wouldn't tolerate his disrespect any longer and that he had to stop referring to me as "she" and to refer to me as "Ms. Simmons" going forward. This courage came from deciding that I would never allow anyone to determine my future again.

7. Write out your dreams.

There's a book by Henriette Anne Klauser entitled *Write It Down, Make It Happen: Knowing What You Want, and Getting It.* There is tangible value in documenting, putting pen to paper or typing on the computer. Seeing your dreams before you, in black and white, makes a big difference.

When you think about it, it's a dream. When you write it down, it becomes a reality. The vision in black-and-white makes it real.

Many people believe what they write, because they see it. We believe what we read, because we can see it. If we write down our dreams and our passions, they will become reality in our own minds.

8. Create your plan.

We must plot out the path to make the dream a reality. Let's say I want to build a house. What is it going to take to build a house? First, lay the foundation. Then, the infrastructure has to be constructed (the electrical wiring, the HVAC units for air conditioning and heating, the plumbing, etc.) Before we erect walls, many things have to be in place.

The same is true for turning our dreams into reality. First, we must determine the foundation we need and consider the investment. Do we need to go back to school for more education? Do we need some specific courses or a certification? To begin gathering the answers, we can do research and identify key people in our industry who might serve as resources. We may volunteer to get hands-on experience so that we can decide whether a particular field or position is right for us. For example, if working for a non-profit is something I believe I want to do, I can look for volunteer opportunities as a way of vetting whether or not this direction is the right one for me.

Reach out to connect with others in the field you are exploring. Start registering for classes. A good friend of mine was able to find free classes to explore one of her talents further. Get in motion; move toward your big dream. The next steps will unfold as you begin to take action.

9. Communicate with your family and supporters.

We must share both our plan and the time frame we anticipate with our family, so they know about the commitment we are making. Openly discuss the adjustments each member of the family needs to make in support of your dream.

When I started my first class, I shared with my husband, "I won't be able to cook every night, because I'll have to make time for not only the class but for study so I do well. Could we share that responsibility?" He was all right with it. We made decisions about how we'd adjust our day-to-day lives as a team. He shared in my dream because I asked him to be a vital part of helping me to make it happen.

Some supporters, colleagues, and friends also may need to be informed, since our commitment may affect our interactions with them.

I had to say "no" to some things. It is hard for most of us to say "no." People ask or insist on our help and we oblige. We have to make saying "no" a good thing for us.

I had to make a few phone calls to say, "You know what? I love your organization. I know I participated and was a principal planner for some of your initiatives. But, in this season, I need to step away."

As long as we do it with respect and honor, it all works out. If the people that you're working with or dealing with care about you, they will understand your priorities and commitments.

I said "no" to somebody I respect and honor. Her response was, "You know what? I am so glad you're telling me 'no'…because that means that you're telling yourself 'yes.'" When I heard her say that, I knew I was doing the right thing.

10. Carve out the time to make it happen.

We must learn to quantify and qualify what we need to do as well as how we invest our time to get those things done. Planning our week allows us to stay on course. We all have the same 24 hours in a day. Learning how to allocate our time and energy is critical for success.

Quantify the hours and time you need for critical activities. Create events or reminders on your electronic calendar to indicate days and times you will focus on specific things. Call and make appointments with people you need to talk to, learn from and brainstorm with. Carve out study times and keep them.

There will be sacrifices that are necessary along the way. We must carve out time for our top priorities and eliminate other things to make room.

Qualify your time by making decisions about what is and isn't important during this season in your life. Watching TV and scrolling through Facebook, Instagram or Twitter may have to take a back seat to your dreams at this time. Hanging out with friends or going shopping may have to be rationed while you are developing your new path in life.

11. Find a trusted mentor.

A mentor is someone who has done what we want to do and is willing to help us walk our path to success. S/he knows the next steps and potential pitfalls, and can help us not only save time but also avoid mistakes that could delay or defer our dream.

Mentors can also make introductions to the right people. Well connected in your industry and seasoned at networking, they are highly valuable allies and guides. I can trace great opportunities that have come my way directly back to trusted mentor relationships.

Next Success Steps

As active women in our communities as well as our homes, we are out trying to make things happen for our children and families. Unfortunately, sometimes we go out without a safety net. One hand is holding the baby, while the other one is making dinner. At the same time, we are focused on making things happen at work.

Know that there is guidance available to help you define your passion and dreams, and to help you make them happen.

You *can* lay out the path forward to the success you want. It requires making a decision and a commitment to yourself and applying lessons learned from the past to your new direction. We must create a clear plan and find the right support to keep moving forward.

If you are at a crossroad right now and are not sure what to do next, let's talk! Go to Women Empowered International on Facebook and connect with me on WomenEmpoweredInternational.com. My email address is Melissa@womenempoweredinternational.com.

We'll schedule your complimentary Success Path Breakthrough session, where we'll discuss what is holding you back from making your dream a reality and identify the number one thing you can do to start turning that around right now.

Remember this: If one door closes, another opens! We just need to be ready to take the right actions to step forward.

About the Author

Melissa Simmons is a graduate of Pace University, where she majored in business administration with a concentration in certified public accounting and a minor in management information systems. Following successful positions in auditing and accounting, she continued her career on the business side of public K-12 education. For 25 years, Melissa has held the positions of controller, budget director and business administrator inside the public education arena.

She is married to the love of her life, Lamont, and is the mother of Ashley, Nicholas and Christian John (aka CJ).

Melissa and her husband are 20-year owners and partners of And2 Marriage Ministries and are authors of the NYCHA "Just Read" award-winning book **The 5 Rules of Marriage**. http://www.and2ministries.org

She is a certified mentor for Women Empowered and is currently working on her dual certification and masters in life and business coaching from Breakthrough and Regent Universities respectively.

Next Success Steps

Dr. Deidre Anderson

Thank you for taking time to read this book. You have made a wise investment. Now, just like the women who shared their stories on these pages, you are poised to come out on the other side of your adversity happier, healthier, wiser, and stronger.

Are you feeling inspired to forge forward and turn your pain into power? Great! We are thrilled that you feel that way.

The truth is, it really does "take a village" of midwives to coach and encourage us as we birth our dreams and transform our lives. Just think about all of the obstacles you have already overcome and the strength that you have gained as a result. Were others there to support you, cheer you on, and pray with you when you experienced tragedies or unexpected circumstances that almost took you out of the game? If we have people like that in our lives, we are truly blessed. Those relationships are priceless.

Yet, there are times we find ourselves contending with curve balls, struggling through challenges or simply wanting to make life changes without anyone there to offer support or understanding.

Remember, you do not have to contend with life's difficulties alone. There is power and value in surrounding yourself with like-minded women who have traveled a similar path, experienced metamorphosis, and come out on the other side ready to extend a hand and help you emerge from your circumstances transformed.

Does your passion to experience transformation require that you act with a sense of urgency? Change your life now by linking arms with these courageous women.

Go to WomenEmpoweredInternational.com and sign up to join us. Also, receive our latest updates and words of inspiration by liking our Women Empowered International page on Facebook (https://www.facebook.com/ Women.Empowered.International).